I'LL TELL YOU WHY...

I CAN'T WEAR THOSE CLOTHES!

TALKING ABOUT TACTILE DEFENSIVENESS

NOREEN O'SULLIVAN

Jessica Kingsley Publishers
London and Philadelphia

First edition published in hardback in Great Britain in 2014 by Jessica Kingsley Publishers

This paperback edition published in Great Britain in 2020 by Jessica Kingsley Publishers
An Hachette Company

1

A CIP catalogue record for this title is available from the British Library and the Library of Congress

ISBN 978 1 78775 662 5

Printed and bound in Great Britain by Ashford Colour Press

Jessica Kingsley Publishers' policy is to use papers that are natural, renewable and recyclable products and made from wood grown in sustainable forests. The logging and manufacturing processes are expected to conform to the environmental regulations of the country of origin.

Jessica Kingsley Publishers
73 Collier Street
London N1 9BE, UK

www.jkp.com

Dedication
To my Mom, for showing me the true meaning of empathy.

Models
Girl – Oona
Puppy – Pippi
Pony – Mini Max

Design
www.mamagraphic.dk
Jeanette Wetche

Photographers
Molly Mort and Noreen O'Sullivan

Photo Editor
www.mamagraphic.dk

I've learned that

people will forget what you said,

people will forget what you did,

but people will never forget
how you made them feel.

Maya Angelou

What do you look like?

In so many ways I'm just like any other kid.

You can't see that my body is not like everyone else's.

What is hard for you to do?

Things that are easy for other kids to do can be really hard for me,
like putting on my clothes and shoes.
It's just that the way things feel can bother me.
So I call it "The Annoying Thing."

Things I like to touch:

Things I don't like to touch:

We all have tiny nerves inside our bodies that we can't see.

They have important jobs to do, like carrying messages from our skin to our brain.

That's how we know when something is soft or hard, or hot or cold.

What annoys you?

Sometimes my nerves send too many messages to my brain.

Suddenly, things can feel too tight, too hot, or just too annoying.

It can really upset and confuse me.

Have you ever felt sad because you couldn't explain how you were feeling?

People don't always understand why I cry or get angry
because they can't see The Annoying Thing.
I wish they knew it was real and that I'm not just trying to be difficult.

Are there things you have to do that you wish weren't so hard?

I wish I could...

take a bath without having to get wet...

What do you think feels too tight?

...put on a seat belt without it feeling so tight...

Are there times that you feel like screaming?

...brush my hair without it hurting so much...

What are your favorite clothes to wear?

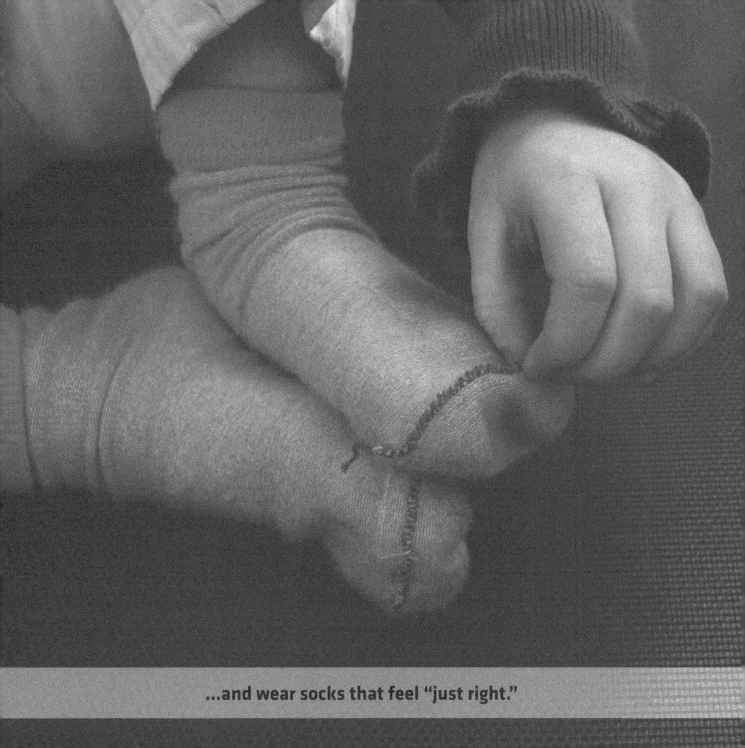

...and wear socks that feel "just right."

Who understands how you feel?

All those things really bother me.

But there are lots of feelings that don't bother me at all

and actually make me happy.

I like to be close to those who understand me.

Can you think of something you need to practice?

There are so many ways for my body to learn about touch,
like baking, painting, and playing with my sensory toys!

What games do you like to play?

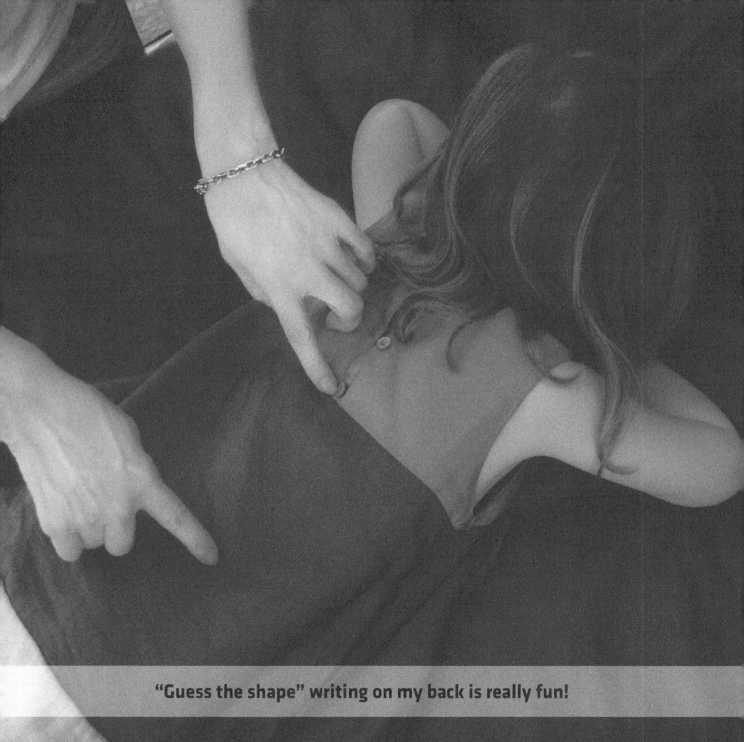

"Guess the shape" writing on my back is really fun!

Are there times when you don't feel like playing a game?

And when my body is not feeling too sensitive,
my favorite game is tickle time with Daddy!

What makes you relax?

There are also many ways for my body to relax.

Foot massages make me feel calm.

The nice feeling from a gentle face massage

stays with me long after Mommy has finished.

Are there days that aren't easy for you?

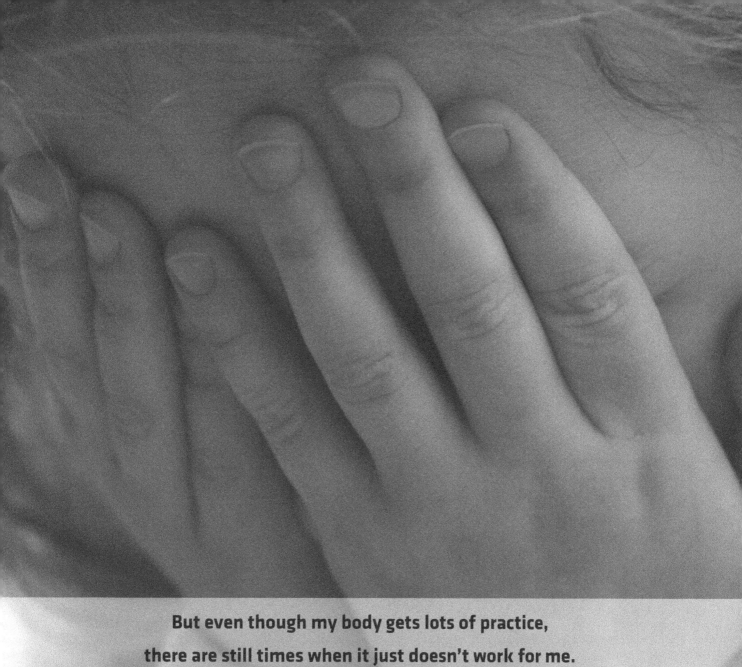

But even though my body gets lots of practice,

there are still times when it just doesn't work for me.

Luckily, there are ways to make those days easier.

What is annoying for you to wear?

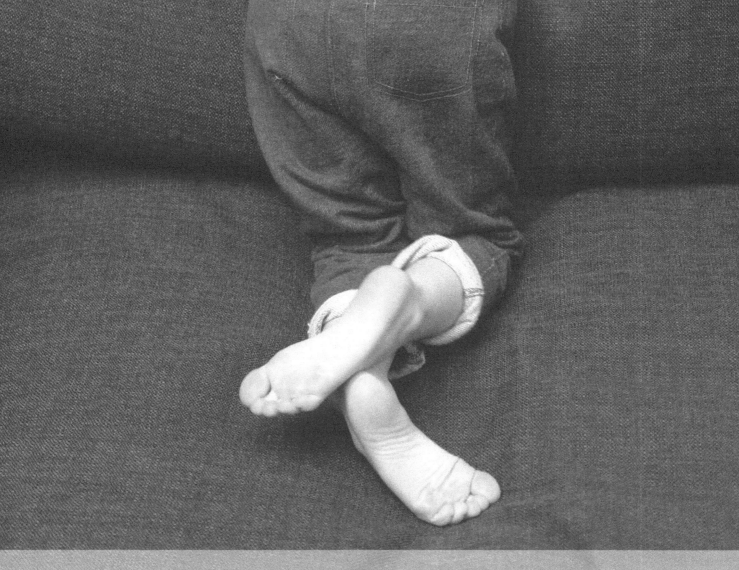

I wear clothes and shoes that are soft and cozy.

I don't like tags, buttons, and thick seams.

My tummy and feet are the most sensitive,

so there are days I just go without socks or underwear.

What sports do you like?

I like sports where I have space around me, and kids don't push and shove.

Do you ever feel different?

I need extra time to get dressed and ready for a new activity.

And it's OK if I do things differently.

What are your favorite healthy foods?

I take care of my body so it can stay happy.

I eat lots of healthy foods like fruits and vegetables.

It's important to give my body lots of water and not too much sugar.

How do you feel when you are tired?

Too many sudden changes and too many plans upset me,

so we try to keep a simple routine for each day.

Those tiny nerves need lots of rest at night, so they can do their job the next day.

Can you remember a time when someone didn't understand why you were upset?

It's not fun when other people don't know about The Annoying Thing.

Sometimes they call me a "cry baby," or think that I just want to decide everything.

I wish they believed me and knew that I would do anything to make it go away.

How do your friends and family help you?

My family and teachers now know that some things really do bother me, and they don't get angry with me so when I say I can't do something. They understand why I like clothes that feel "just right."

What makes you feel better?

There are still many days when I scream and cry if something is annoying.

But now the people around me try to help me when that happens,

because they know my feelings are real.

A gentle hug sure does feel better than an angry yell.

Note to Parents and Teachers

This book addresses the emotional isolation and daily struggles felt by children with **TACTILE DEFENSIVENESS**. It does not aim to treat or diagnose the dysfunction. Awareness is rapidly growing, yet many doctors, teachers and other professionals are not familiar with the topic.

If you suspect your child suffers from tactile defensiveness it is important to find an experienced, licensed and registered **OCCUPATIONAL THERAPIST** and an **INTEGRATIVE NUTRIONALIST** who seek to find a holistic and drug-free approach to treatment. Keep a journal of your child's behavior and physical well-being. Note connections between tummy ache, skin rashes, ear ache, etc. when behavior is extreme. Pay close attention to food reactions (egg, dairy, soy and wheat in particular) and their effects on your child.

About the Author

This book is inspired by the personal experiences of my daughters and my own quest to have their voices heard.

Having worked for many years as an elementary school teacher, my goal is to provide emotional advocacy for all children.
The voices of so many misunderstood children deserve to be heard and accepted.

This book is an introduction to accepting your child's sensitivities.
For **MORE** understanding and treatments visit these sites:

www.spdconnect.com - support group for parents of sensitive children
www.softclothing.net - clothing for sensitive children
www.craniosacraltherapy.org - light touch massage for children
www.eagala.org - horse therapy for children
www.jkp.com/catalogue/book/9781843108627 - a book on yoga poses for children with tactile issues
www.sensory-processing-disorder.com - knowledge and support group
www.sensorysmart.co.uk - children's clothing in Europe
www.itmakessense.com.au - children's clothing in Australia
www.seamsaway.com.au - children's clothing in Australia
www.wholenewmom.com - recipes and healthy living ideas for parents
www.drhyman.com - functional medicine doctor for healthy living
www.greatplainslaboratory.com - food intolerances testing lab
www.yummly.com - food recipe bank with allergy/special diet adaptations
www.unicorn.dk/english/index.html - color and relax mandalas for children
www.mindbodygreen.com - MOST IMPORTANT! Taking care of yourself

Your own feelings

_____

_____

_____

_____

_____

_____

_____

_____

_____